The Bronx:
Three Memoirs

W. R. Rodriguez

zeugpress

Acknowledgments:

These articles were written for *The Bronx County Historical Society Journal,* to which I have granted non-exclusive reprint rights. They were written, years apart, as separate pieces, so a few details may repeat themselves. Although his family also lived in the South Bronx, my father died long before I began writing these reminiscences, which are based on my memories and on those of my mother. I do miss the stories Dad could have told.

"138th Street and Brook Avenue," © 1996 W. R. Rodriguez, appeared in *The Bronx County Historical Society Journal:* Volume XXXIII, Number 2, Fall 1996.

"My Mother's Life in Mott Haven," © 2000 W. R. Rodriguez, appeared in *The Bronx County Historical Society Journal*: Volume XXXVII, Number 1, Spring 2000.

"Fordham," © 2016 W. R. Rodriguez, appeared in *The Bronx County Historical Society Journal:* Volume LIV, Numbers 1 & 2, Spring/Fall 2017.

☙

© 2016 W. R. Rodriguez

All rights reserved

ISBN: 978-0-9632201-5-8

Printed in the United States of America

zeugpress

Contents

My Mother's Life in Mott Haven 5

138th Street and Brook Avenue 16

Fordham 40

Publications by W. R. Rodriguez 62

To Mom, with love.

My Mother's Life in Mott Haven

My mother was born on Eighth Avenue, the last child in a family of eleven, nine of whom survived. One died of measles and one of influenza. Her father had arrived in America as a young boy. His father, who was in the exporting business, died on a trip to Italy, and my grandfather was raised in America by an aunt and an uncle. He returned to Italy to serve in the army, married a woman who worked on the family farm, and brought his wife to America where they started a family. He saved up enough money to buy a shoeshine parlor near the corner of 138th Street and Brook Avenue in The Bronx. The bootblack business provided a basic income to support this large family. It gave my grandfather and my uncles the flexibility to work other jobs, and the family survived the booms and busts of the 1920s and the 1930s. Even in my generation it was a rite of passage for the boys to be taken into the business. The shoeshine parlor remained in the family until the mid-1970s when my uncle retired and sold it. By then, most of the family had moved from Mott Haven.

Mom's earliest memory is of that day in 1925 when the family moved from Manhattan to The Bronx: the moving man yelled at her and her brother, who were jumping on the mattress. The family settled in at 535 East 134th Street. Between Brook and Saint Ann's Avenues, 134th Street consisted of private houses and tenements, a small cookie factory, and a dairy. The apartment was a cold-water flat that had a coal stove in the kitchen. There was one bedroom for the boys, one for the girls, and one for the parents. With so many girls crammed into one bed, Mom often snuck into the living room to sleep on the sofa bed. In the summers this was the coolest room, so sometimes there was competition for this choice spot, but Mom argued that she had priority because she often slept there in the winter when it was the coldest room. Being the youngest, she did not always win.

Sharing the boys' room was Uncle Giaco. Giaco had immigrated to America, and a relative was supposed to meet him at the dock. When the ship landed no one was there to meet him. Somehow he met my grandfather, who took him in, and he became an honorary uncle. He worked in the shoeshine parlor and lived with our family for the rest of his life. Giaco returned to Italy once to visit his relatives; despite his American citizenship, he was told that he would be drafted into the Italian army. He had served as a runner for General Pershing in the United States Army during World War I, so he remained on the boat and did not set foot on Italian soil. He never tried to return to Italy after that. In 1954, while crossing 138th Street to buy ice cream, he was struck down by an automobile. He is buried in the family grave at Saint Raymond's Cemetery.

My mother's childhood in The Bronx during the 1920s and 1930s is still vivid in her memory. Doors were left unlocked; sometimes the milkman left the milk inside the door. There were few cars, and children could walk to school or to the park without worrying their parents. Mom and one of her brothers sometimes walked miles to visit their aunt; they followed the trolley tracks up Saint Ann's Avenue and went crosstown on 149th Street. On one of these wanderings Mom and her brother stayed too long fishing and crabbing on the docks of the Harlem River. They arrived home after dark, and my grandfather was so angry that he threatened to get out the belt. Mom dashed into the bedroom and hid under the bed for the rest of the night. Her brother simply handed over the crabs which were promptly cooked and eaten amid laughter and conversation. But Mom played it safe and did not venture out for a snack.

Harvesting the local waterways for fish, crabs, or eels was not the only way the family stretched its budget. The rail yards were searched for lumps of coal that had fallen from trains, and wood was gathered from discarded boxes; these gleanings were consumed by the stove that warmed the cold-water flat. Mom and one of her brothers often sold shopping bags and newspapers. They saved the money they earned and treated themselves to candy and to Saturday afternoon movies. A lucrative part of their business was selling the evening papers, but this was squelched when a policeman complained that they were too young to be out after dark. After that, they simply sold shopping bags on 137th Street.

Between Brook and Saint Ann's Avenues, 137th Street had an interior market complex consisting of fruit and vegetable stands, a butcher shop, and a delicatessen, which Mom remembers for its barrels of sauerkraut and pickles. On the corner of Brook Avenue there was a large Jewish delicatessen and restaurant that made magnificent sandwiches. 137th Street was lined with outdoor peddlers and with many stores. One was a poultry market with live chickens in crates. Her mother would feel the chickens' chests to see if they were tender. Once the meal was picked, the butcher would kill it. A rabbi was often on the scene to ensure that the meat was kosher. An Italian store near Brook Avenue sold various pasta, which was stored in large drawers and sold by the pound. Serving the Italian, Irish, German, and Jewish immigrants, 137th Street had the flavor of an international marketplace.

Eventually the building at 535 East 134th Street was condemned; the residents were told that it was leaning. The family moved again, to 531 East 134th Street. This apartment had electricity and steam heat; there was no need to fill a stove with coal. Eventually the entire street was condemned to provide access to the Triborough Bridge. So in the late 1920s the family moved once more, to 526 East 138th Street. Grandfather was considering moving to a private home in the Pelham Bay area, but Grandmother insisted that he live near his work. He owned a shoeshine parlor on the corner of 138th and Brook, and bartended at the Paradise Bar on Brook Avenue, so 138th Street was a convenient location.

My grandfather died in 1938 and, as was the custom, was laid out for five days in the living room. As a bootblack and a bartender, he was well known in the neighborhood; both the living room and the dining room were filled with flowers. Over the years, Mom's siblings married and moved out to start families of their own. Three of her sisters took apartments on 138th Street, so this large family remained close. After her mother died, Mom got married and remained in the apartment until 1970, when we moved to the Fordham area.

Having spent forty-five years in Mott Haven, and having lived all but two of her seventy-seven years in The Bronx, Mom is a true Bronxite with a passion for nostalgia. She grew up in an era of low crime, when The Bronx was a wonderland to be explored and enjoyed. As a child she once walked her niece, who fortunately was in a stroller, all the way to Bronx Park and back. Another time she took her niece to the Willis Avenue Bridge; Mom liked to eat lunch there and to watch the bridge open to allow boats to pass. Mom and her mother often walked over the bridge on their way to shop in Harlem or to visit Our Lady of Mount Carmel Church on 116th Street. This church was a favorite of the Italians and held a big feast every summer. Even when I was a young child we walked to the festival and stopped for pizza at Patsy's on the way back. It was quite a trek, but the pizza, Italian ices, and zeppoles (deep-fried dough sprinkled with confectioner's sugar) made it worthwhile.

The Triborough Bridge was also quite an attraction. Visiting relatives were taken to see this architectural wonder. Mom remembers Roosevelt visiting to celebrate its opening. My grandfather, a devout Democrat, ran out to the caravan to shake his hand. He knew most of the neighborhood police, so he did not get in trouble. The bridge provided a cool place to walk on hot summer nights, and it offered a wonderful view of the Manhattan skyline. It also offered access to Randall's Island, which became a favorite spot for weekend picnics. On weekdays it was a peaceful and spacious place for the children to play.

When Mom grew up, toys were not abundant. A girl might own one doll, maybe two. Childhood games did not require much more than jump ropes, jacks, or marbles. A baseball or football might be manufactured out of rags; a broomstick might do for a bat. Carts or scooters could be made from scrap wood and wheels. Games such as tag, red rover, ringolevio, or Johnny-on-the-pony did not require any equipment at all. As she grew older, Mom could save up for a softball glove or roller skates. She loved sports. As a teen she walked up to Kelly Street to play on a softball team. Despite the freedom to wander, curfews were strict. Mom was not allowed to talk to boys in the street, and there were always plenty of older brothers around to enforce this rule. The police did not allow loitering. Children were allowed to play in the streets, but the police often told teenagers to move along, even if they were standing on the stoops of the buildings where they lived.

Like most immigrants struggling to make it in America during the 1920s and 1930s, the family had a strong work ethic, and the children were expected to contribute. The boys worked at the shoeshine parlor until they got older and married and took other jobs. Mom was given the specialty jobs like cleaning white shoes or doing the two-tone shoes; this was time-consuming and meticulous work. After Uncle Giaco died, Uncle Al kept the shoeshine parlor going. He worked it mornings (after his night shift at the Railroad Express Agency) and weekends; he employed his nephews and other neighborhood kids. When he retired he sold the shanty, which was converted into a newsstand. Sneakers, sandals, and synthetic leather had taken their toll on patronage; the era of the bootblack had passed.

Children were responsible for helping with the housework. Mom and her brother had to carry the Oriental rug up to the roof, hang it up, and beat it clean. On Saturday mornings the leather couch had to be cleaned with lemon oil. The girls who did not like cleaning had to walk to the stores and help carry the bundles. Cooking was a time-consuming and labor-intensive process, but it maintained the family's ties to the Old World. Chickens had to be plucked and rabbits cleaned before they could be cooked. Tomato sauce was made from scratch. Tomato paste was left in a box on the fire escape to dry; a cheesecloth kept the flies off, and it was occasionally uncovered to be drained and stirred. Dough was made, flattened on bed sheets, stuffed, and cut with a fork into ravioli to be dried and boiled.

For special occasions Grandfather bought bunches of grapes to make wine, but there were plenty of kids around to nibble at the grapes before they could be pressed and fermented. Homemade sausages were hung from a line in the kitchen. Every Sunday the family gathered for a big meal. Even during the Depression, Grandmother managed to provide this for her family. And during wartime, one of my uncles might bring his shipmates or other servicemen to the feast. After the big Sunday meal, the family relaxed by playing cards. The radio offered its fare of entertainment: music, serials, and ball games.

One of my mother's favorite childhood pastimes was the movies. For new releases Mom went to Loew's National or RKO Royal near 149th Street. The least expensive seats were in the upper balcony, which the kids called "seventh heaven" because it was so high up. Those going to the balcony used a separate entrance, but for a quarter they saw two movies and a stage show. First runs were on Friday, Saturday, and Sunday. Older films were shown on Monday and Tuesday, and another set of second runs was shown on Wednesday and Thursday. The neighborhood also had many second run theaters. The Peerless, across from the 40th precinct, was one of the theaters that the children called a "flea joint" because ushers walked around with flit guns and sprayed the bugs. It was not very appealing, but admission was only a nickel. Mom went there if she did not have the dime charged by many of the other local theaters. In addition to flit guns, The Bronx Opera House, at 149th Street near

Brook Avenue, featured cats that ran through the rows of seats. Mom was never fond of cats and sat with her feet up. She and her brothers only went there if they got free passes, which they sometimes did in return for putting up posters at the shoeshine parlor of the theater's upcoming events.

Mom's favorite theater was the Forum at 138th Street and Brown Place. She went there almost every Saturday. For ten cents she received four hours of entertainment: two movies, cartoons, newsreels, and a serial. A trip to Grant's or to Woolworth's Five and Ten beforehand provided a pound of candy for a dime; the kids pooled their goodies and passed them around during the show. Mom was at the Forum when the show was stopped and a man walked on the stage to announce that the Lindbergh baby had been kidnapped. It was in the Forum that Mom saw her first talkie; she remembers Al Jolson singing "My Mammy" in *The Jazz Singer*.

When she got older she often went to the Casino at 138th and Willis. It offered vaudeville acts, amateur nights, and bingo. One of her brothers sometimes helped change the letters on the marquee. Mom held the ladder and passed the letters up to him. In return, they got free admission. The Casino was still running double features when I was a child. The Oceola, at 139th Street and St. Ann's Avenue, offered silent movies accompanied by an organist. The doors were left open in the summer, and there was an outdoor theater adjacent to it. When Mom was in junior high school, she often stayed home from school on Friday afternoons because of stomach aches, possibly caused by fear of an unkind teacher. The Oceola featured cowboy movies on Fridays, and sometimes her brother took her along.

Mom went to elementary school at PS 43 on Brown Place and 135th Street. While waiting to get in, the students used to pile up their books and see how many stacks of books they could jump over. Sometimes the kids played tag at lunchtime, and sometimes

Mom would run home for a cup of tea. There was a dress code and Mom had to wear a dark blue skirt and a white middy blouse with a blue scarf (red scarves for assembly days). In junior high the uniform was similar: blue skirt, white blouse, and stockings; anklets were not permitted. At Wilton Junior High, on 141st Street between Brook and Saint Ann's Avenues, discipline was strict. No playing was allowed outside school; students lined up and went in silently. Passing time was done in silent double file. The school was all girls and was let out a few minutes before Clark Junior High, an all-boys' school, was dismissed. The teachers were old and seemed unpleasant; Mom likened the overall atmosphere to that of a reform school.

After graduating from Wilton, Mom attended Central Commercial High School on 42nd Street next to the Daily News Building. The teachers were terrific and treated the students like human beings. They were young and friendly. Mom loved it there and cried when she graduated. She enjoyed art and wanted to take art courses. Mom was very disappointed that the art program was moved to the annex. Mom decided to stay at the main school and took clerical courses. She studied bookkeeping, typing, and filing, and she learned to use the office machines of the time. Mom graduated in 1940 and was the only one of her family to receive a high school diploma. A few months after graduation, Mom started her first job in a five-and-ten store. She worked forty-eight hours a week, no overtime, no benefits, and holidays were deducted from the paycheck. It was 1940 and she made $14.50 a week.

Mom has always been an avid Yankees fan. Mom almost saw Babe Ruth play, but she got home from school too late and her father took one of her sisters to the game instead. When she was ten or eleven, she attended Sunday doubleheaders with her oldest brother. He was a policeman working the vice squad in plainclothes. Mom suspects that he was there to keep track of the bookies. He would sit her down and go off to do his work. He would occasionally return to check on her and to bring her ice cream. When she was in high school she attended ladies' days: a quarter admission for any seat in the house; this eventually changed in the 1940s, and the women were relegated to the grandstands. The morning session at Commercial High let out at noon, so on Fridays Mom and her friends headed uptown to the ballpark. If the Yankees were on the road, the Giants were at the Polo Grounds. One of her teachers knew Lou Gehrig and they often sat with her behind the Yankees dugout. After the games the fans could run onto the field. Once Mom got close enough to Joe DiMaggio to ask for his autograph; he was just about to take her pencil and sign her scorecard, but a policeman intervened and moved the fans away. She has never forgotten that brief moment with one of her heroes.

Mom not only enjoyed watching sports, she also loved participating in them. The girls in her high school class would get together and play softball in the schoolyard of PS 52. She joined the PAL and began playing on a girls' basketball team. After high school she got a job at S. S. Kresge & Company Five & Ten on 106th street. She began roller-skating with her coworkers at the rink on 188th and Park. Even when the other ladies lost interest in the sport, she continued. Gay Blades, on 52nd Street near Broadway, was often crowded with servicemen. The Fordham Skating Rink had curved edges, so it was not one of her favorites. When she came home after an evening of roller-skating, she always stopped in Jake's candy store at 518 East 138th Street. Jake would let her in, even at closing time, which was at 11 or 11:30, and make her a big malt or an ice-cream soda piled with whipped cream. He thought she was too skinny and needed the extra calories. Mom was quite active. She was up at five, off to work, home for dinner, out to skating, and in bed at midnight. The subways and streets were safe, the Depression was over, and, for those who were not going to war, life in The Bronx was fun.

After leaving the five-and-ten she got a job at Burndy's Engineering on 132nd Street off Brown Place. America had entered the war, and she replaced a man who had entered the service. She was a file clerk in the pattern shop, the only woman in that department. Burndy's was part of the great arsenal of democracy. Parts were made for tanks, ships, airplanes, for anything that moved. Patterns were formed in wood; a mold was made, cast in the foundry, then cleaned and finished in the shop. Eventually the building was condemned so that a highway could be built. The offices remained on 132nd Street for a few more years, and Mom remained there as a clerk in the standards department. Finally, the offices moved to Connecticut. Burndy's foundry and the pattern shop were moved to 137th and Jackson. Ultimately these too left The Bronx. As far as we know, the proposed highway was never built and the original Burndy's building is still standing today. Mom stopped working at Burndy's when I was born. She still has a small bust of MacArthur and a pair of bronze dogs that some of the workers cast between other jobs. She has always been fascinated by the craftsmanship of the men she worked with.

After a bad knee put an end to Mom's roller-skating, she began to date my father. They went to movies, Yankees games, and dances. They frequented the old Madison Square Garden, which hosted hockey, rodeos, boxing, horse shows, wrestling, and the Harvest Moon Ball. They liked to go to Ranger games and root for the opponents. They had season tickets for the Devils' hockey games and often rooted for the opponents as well. During a playoff game Mom's rooting for the Boston team angered the fans in the row in front of her. Words were exchanged and someone took a swing at my uncle but hit his young son instead. The Boston fans sitting behind Mom lent a hand, and the ensuing scuffle caused the players to stop the game in order to watch it.

A boxing match between Joe Louis and Jersey Joe Walcott ended in a near riot when fans began throwing chairs at the ring; fortunately, Mom and Dad were sitting in the upper tier and were able to leave before the crowd got too out of hand. They enjoyed taking cruises, but the war put a damper on that. They often sailed up the Hudson on the Saturday moonlight cruise, which offered onboard dancing. Once, for a change of pace, they took a Saturday-night excursion to New Jersey. As they stood on deck Mom noticed that there was another ship ahead of them. Mom wondered why it was there, and Dad explained that it was opening up the mine fields so the cruise ship could pass. It made Mom nervous, and that was her last cruise for a while.

After I was born in the early 1950s, Mom left her job and spent her time raising her only child. I grew up in the apartment her parents had moved to in the late 1920s. Often accompanied by my cousins and my aunt, Mom and I made frequent trips to St. Mary's Park, Randall's Island, Astoria Pool, and The Bronx Zoo. For movies we went to the Casino, the theaters at the Hub, and occasionally to the awe-inspiring Loew's Paradise. There were frequent walks to Alexander's at the Hub; to us youngsters this seemed like quite a long journey. When we moved to the Fordham area in 1970, Mom was delighted to be just a couple of blocks from an Alexander's. Shopping there became her hobby. She visited it many times a week, almost every day it seemed, getting exercise and hunting for bargains.

Mom has seen The Bronx change greatly; she has lived through urban blight and urban renewal. She is a true Bronxite who loves the noise, the traffic, the people, the sirens, the general excitement. And when the Yankees win in October she is in absolute ecstasy. Of all her memories of how The Bronx has changed, of how her favorite theaters, bakeries, ice-cream parlors, five-and-tens, candy stores, and pizza parlors have almost all disappeared, the saddest loss by far is the closing of Alexander's. Like many other Bronxites, she has never completely recovered.

138th Street and Brook Avenue

Sometime during the 1920s my grandfather brought a shoeshine parlor on the southeast corner of 138th Street and Brook Avenue. My grandfather was an Italian immigrant who had moved from Philadelphia to Manhattan, then to a tenement on 134th Street in the South Bronx; when it was razed to make way for the Major Deegan Expressway, he settled on 138th Street so that he could be near his business. Nine of his eleven children survived childhood, and four of his five daughters rented apartments on 138th Street where they raised their own families. The American dream of a house in the country was not a possibility for them; surviving the Depression and paying the bills was enough. It was their children who made the great exodus to the suburbs.

I grew up with a sense of family that I will probably never experience again. There were fourteen cousins of a variety of ages distributed among 514, 522, and 526 East 138th Street. There was always someone for the kids to play with, and there was always something for the adults to talk about. On summer afternoons the mothers gathered, leaning on parked cars or sitting on milk crates, and watched as we played. On hot summer nights the fathers joined them. I was born in 1953, and I lived on 138th Street until 1971. The '50s and '60s saw many changes in national and local politics; the Cuban Missile Crisis prompted worried conversations about a cousin in the navy; the Kennedy assassination was a mortal shock; Mayor Lindsay provided anger and amusement. But much of the talk was centered on the family and the neighborhood: Who was arguing? Who was getting married? Who was moving? Where was there to move?

The South Bronx itself experienced a fair amount of change. Tenements were condemned, torn down, and housing projects were erected. A carnival was held on the lot where the Millbrook Projects would be built. My parents never trusted the safety of the rides in these itinerant carnivals, but there were booths with gaming wheels that we loved to play. Someone won a plaster clown, which we filled with pennies. Because of the Millbrooks, it was no longer possible to see the Manhattan skyline from the window of my aunt's apartment, a rear one which overlooked the roof of the 137th Street market. But the projects had open space, and when we were fairly young Mom let us sneak in to enjoy the new playground. After the Millbrooks were completed, more projects were put up between Willis and Third Avenues. When my mother took me to the A&P we often stopped to look at the enormous holes which were to hold the foundations of those tall buildings. The wonderful pizza parlor on Willis Avenue, and the friends who had lived in the razed tenements, would never return to the neighborhood.

Mom took me in a stroller to watch the tearing-down of the southern section of the Third Avenue El. Years later, during my first semester at Fordham University, I often took the Willis Avenue bus or walked to 149th Street and caught the El. The cars were vintage; I think that they still had straw seats and ceiling fans, and if someone almost missed the train, the doors could be pried open by hand. Through the windows of the shaking cars one could get a panorama of the central Bronx. During my second semester of college, we moved to an apartment just off Fordham Road, so my commuting days on the Third Avenue El were over. One night, in the spring of 1973, as I was walking along Southern Boulevard, I saw a transit policeman padlock the Bedford Station; the El had made its last run.

I began my long education at PS 43, which was on Brown Place and 135th Street—the same school my mother had attended. Some of my cousins had attended PS 9, but I was not slated to go there. PS 9 was quite old and eventually burned down; the fire department supervised the scene for three days. After the school was demolished, the remaining lot became an asphalt park. In the auditorium of PS

43 there was a mural depicting settlers and Indians; I later figured out that this must have been a rendering of Jonas Bronck's settling of the area; the school bore his name. The space program was new, and the teachers gathered us in the auditorium to watch one of the blastoffs. There was a lengthy delay, so we were allowed to watch *My Little Margie.* Across the street was a 600 school, which we were told was for juvenile delinquents. Its schoolyard was a cement valley surrounded by towering fences; we never saw anyone outside. In fourth grade I was sent to PS 31 to be part of the academically accelerated program. I took the subway to school; it seemed to be faster than the bus. William Lloyd Garrison Elementary School at 144th and the Grand Concourse was a fascinating building which looked like a modified castle; the entrance, about fifteen feet above street level, was up a flight of stairs; the entire building was surrounded by iron bars. There was a large playground adjacent to it, and we spent our lunch periods playing on the monkey bars, the punchball field, or the handball court.

My class was sent to Arturo Toscanini Junior High, a new school that was just opening. I had to take two buses to get to 165th Street and Clay Avenue. Construction of the school had not been completed; books and supplies were not ready, and we attended part-time for three months until a regular school day could be offered. We were to complete three years of junior high in two years, and we lost much of our seventh grade education. Chaos reigned. A group of students walked into our math class and beat up a girl, presumably because she helped our homeroom teacher grade papers. Our homeroom teacher, a short young lady with a feisty spirit, was threatened by students, was in at least one fight, and had had her car vandalized. She was well liked by our class, and I was especially indebted to her because she discreetly rescued me from a gang of ten boys who were going to beat me up because I happened to look like another boy who was running for class president against a popular girl. After one year, our class was transferred to another school. I was glad that I would not have to return to such chaos.

We were promoted from seventh grade to ninth and sent to Wade Junior High School, just off the Concourse at 176th Street. Another subway trip. The principal was not nice to us; half of our class was Black or Hispanic; I suspect that was the reason we were not welcome. In order to make up for the education we lost in seventh grade, we were required to stay for after-school tutoring. Near the end of the first semester, half of our class, mostly minorities, were sent back to their neighborhood schools and put back in eighth grade. The one "white" student who was removed from the gifted program was allowed to stay in ninth grade at Wade. There was no sensitivity in the handling of the matter; the principal merely came into our class one afternoon and read the names of those students who were to be shipped out. One girl ran down the hallway in tears. I was on the list but my angry father advocated for me; I remained at Wade and graduated from ninth grade, one of sixteen survivors from a class of thirty-two, most of whom had started in the academically-advanced program in fourth grade.

In seventh grade I and several other students had been told that we had passed the test for Bronx High School of Science. But we were sent to Wade for ninth grade. At the end of ninth grade we were told that if we attended summer school and if we improved our grades, we might be admitted into Science. There were too many "ifs" for this Bronx boy, so I chose to go to DeWitt Clinton. I never regretted it. The school was ethnically mixed and everyone seemed to get along. I soon worked my way into the honors classes, and then into scholarship classes. DeWitt Clinton had an excellent academic program; the reading list in my eleventh-grade English class probably equaled that of many a freshman college course. Clinton also offered general and vocational diplomas; it was indeed a school for everyone, except girls.

Clinton officially had about eight thousand students, all boys. Gym was the largest class; about three hundred boys lined up in rows for attendance check in the big gymnasium. One had to pass four years of gym in order to graduate, so there was little fooling around; discipline was handled by zero period: a punishment gym class at seven a.m. Class began with a mandatory run around the elevated track; there were monitors posted to report dawdlers who tried to linger on the staircase. We often had stampedes in which fifty or so students decided to simultaneously accelerate the running pace, causing everyone ahead to do so as well.

Since I was too short to play basketball, I spent much of my time on this track, jogging away the period in my Converse sneakers. I spent some time in the swimming pool, a fun alternative to regular gym, and was glad to learn that we were the first class allowed to wear bathing suits. We had to rent the suits from the school, and after a few weeks the strings and elastic wore out from the frequent washings, so we were asked to bring diaper pins. Some of our races had surprise endings when a bathing suit wound up around someone's ankles.

The school day began with a long subway ride. As the Woodlawn proceeded north, more and more Clinton boys accumulated on the train. Underclassmen had the late shift, from 11:15 to 4:45. In the afternoon, we had to cross Mosholu Parkway during rush hour to get to the El station; we gathered in a large crowd, and when there were enough of us we swarmed the street, defying the cars. Seniors had the early shift; I was able to get to work in Manhattan by two-thirty. This was helpful, as I was saving money for college.

Thanks to having completed junior high in two years, I graduated from high school when I was sixteen. Thanks to the academic preparation I received at DeWitt Clinton, I was awarded a Regents Scholarship and was accepted for admission to Fordham University. Half of my tuition would be paid for by scholarship; my father and I would split the rest. I could live at home so there was no extra expense for room and board. I still cherish my years at Fordham; they were the pleasant highlight of my genuine Bronx education.

Until the end of my first semester of college, when we moved from the South Bronx, we lived in the apartment where Mom had lived since childhood. Her father died in 1938, and her mother in 1948. Mom married my father in 1950, and he moved in. I was born a few years later, and inherited a bedroom once inhabited by various relatives who had gone off to establish their own families. And I inherited a neighborhood where my family had deep roots.

The corners of 138th Street and Brook Avenue featured a drug store, a candy store, a cigar store, and an ice-cream parlor which became Ted's shoe store. My folks never used the corner pharmacy; they preferred the one which was on Brook Avenue. It was a thrill to visit on hot summer days—the air conditioning was chilling. There were not many toys to look at, and not much candy, but the telephone booth had folding doors and it was fun to sit in it while waiting for prescriptions to be filled. The cigar store was much more fascinating. It offered a substantial candy rack and it sold baseball cards. When I had the chicken pox, I was cheered up by the acquisition of a Mickey Mantle card in a pack of Topps. I wish I still had it today.

The candy store itself had a large collection of comics; *Superman* and *Batman* were popular, but I also had an interest in *Archie, Sad Sack, GI Joe, The Fantastic Four,* and *Spiderman*. I liked *Mad Magazine,* but my mother did not approve of it. As I grew older I often joined the crowd that waited for the twilight edition of *The Daily News*. For me, it was something to do: wait for the paper. Many of the others waiting were interested in the racing results and in the reporting of the total pari-mutuel handle: the last three digits were the number. At the time, there were no state lotteries or Off Track Betting. Aside from the bookies, there was the annual Irish Sweepstakes and bingo, but that was it.

The ice-cream parlor closed when I was quite young. It was a great loss, not only because of the disappearance of its treats, but because my uncle could no longer use its basement. He had a deal with the owner: my uncle swept and shoveled the sidewalk; in return, he could use the cellar, the entrance to which was just a few feet from his shoeshine parlor. The basement was a clubhouse of sorts. There was a pool table, a dartboard, a bathroom, and a shower made from a coffin. My uncle and my older cousins gathered there on Friday and Saturday nights. I got to visit a few times and was in awe of it all. But by the time I was old enough to shine shoes, the shoe store had taken the basement, which it needed for its inventory.

There were many places to eat in the neighborhood. An inexpensive favorite was Bill's frankfurter store. For twenty-five cents one could get a special: hot dog, fries, and soda. Bill's sold pizza and bottles of soda—Nehi was my favorite—and there were bottle caps all over the street. We collected them and nailed them onto scooters that were constructed from old roller skates and wooden milk boxes, or we filled the caps with melted Crayolas and used them as "shooters" in a game that we called sidewalk checkers. We even got magnets and fished bottle caps out of the subway gratings, just for the fun of it. Sometimes coins had fallen into the gratings beneath the parking meters. We applied a wad of heated bubble gum or a glob of petroleum jelly to our magnets and tried to "catch" a coin. It was not easy. The final challenge was to get the coin through the grille without it shaking loose. Much of the sport went out of subway-grating fishing when one or two of the neighborhood boys jumped the turnstiles and climbed into the airspace from below; they could take whatever money they could find as long as they were able to dodge the authorities.

Our section of 138th Street had clothing stores, a jewelry store, shoe stores, a delicatessen, a butcher shop, a barber's, furniture stores, restaurants, and bars. At Christmas the merchants had lights hung across the thoroughfare; it was always a treat to see them turned on at those early winter sunsets. Across the street were two five-and-tens: Grant's and Woolworth's. Woolworth's had many toys, and I enjoyed looking at model kits for the plastic airplanes and cars that I loved to build and to paint. It was a longstanding family tradition to take pictures outside of Grant's; the store appears in many of our old photographs.

When Mom wanted to shop for clothes, she went to 149th Street; the area was known as the Hub. It seemed like a long walk, but she usually bought me a pretzel at Hearn's or at the five-and-ten. Alexander's was her store of preference. We spent hours there. When we finally moved from the South Bronx in 1971, we relocated just off Fordham Road, only two blocks from an even larger Alexander's. Alexander's was very much a part of our lives. Many Saturdays my father drove us out to Rego Park in Queens. We even ventured once to the New Jersey store and a couple of times to the Alexander's in Connecticut. When I was a teenager, I worked on the Upper East side of Manhattan; after I got paid on Friday or Saturday nights I often walked down to the 59th Street Alexander's to check out the record sales or to buy jeans. After years of living near Fordham Road, my mother got to know many of the salesladies. It was a great loss when the Alexander's chain closed.

Not nearly as long as the trips to Alexander's but more frequent were the grocery trips. The two nearest A&Ps were at Cypress Avenue and at Willis Avenue; both seemed so far away when we were young. I was glad when an E&B opened on Saint Ann's Avenue at 139th Street. It was much closer, and I had a profitable business venture going: my aunt let me return all her family's soda and beer bottles. At a nickel each I could make two or three dollars each trip; it seemed like a fortune.

In the summers my mother did her best to keep me entertained. The Casino, a second-run movie theater on Willis Avenue, showed double features. The Loew's National and the RKO Royal were near the Hub. Once we went to the Casino on a Wednesday afternoon; the movies changed at five o'clock and we stayed for the third show and for a good part of the fourth: almost eight hours in a theater for one admission. The first movie Mom took me to was *Bambi;* we went to the RKO Fordham, and we stood on line for an hour in the rain. The Paradise was always a treat; the stars on the ceiling fascinated me. When I graduated from DeWitt Clinton in 1970, the ceremony was held at the Paradise. Our well-rehearsed entrance lines were broken when some of the boys stopped to give their boutonnieres to girls who happened to be sitting near the aisles. On Brown Place was a theater called the Puerto Rico; it had once been the Forum. Since I did not speak Spanish, I never went there. It offered shows as well as movies, and the lines often extended to 137th Street. One summer a small circus was there. Two baby elephants and a donkey took up temporary residence in the alley off Brook Avenue.

Many times my mother and my aunt took us to Astoria Pool. There was a long walk to Jackson Avenue, a restless wait for the bus, a scenic trip across the Triborough Bridge, then another long walk from the bus to the park. If we arrived early, there was a very long line waiting for the pool to open. But we usually stayed there for the entire day, so it was worth it. When my skin shriveled and when my cousins started to turn blue, our mothers made us go to the concession stand, where we bought candy and a chocolate drink called Yoo-hoo. The eating area overlooked the War Memorial and the Hell Gate. Once one of my cousins put his head through the metal bars; he was fairly skinny and liked to impress us by wiggling through the accordion gates of some of the local shops. But he could not get his head out of these bars, not without the help of the fire department. The bent iron amused us in future visits.

Astoria had three pools. The diving pool had a tall concrete diving tower, which was not open to the general public, and some shorter diving platforms. There was a shallow wading pool for toddlers— it had a very slippery bottom. The main pool was huge, and if we stayed long enough we could see the underwater lights; their beams emanated not only from the four sides, but also from structures built into the middle of the pool; the effect was surreal. The bus ride home seemed endless, but we often got some candy from the concession stands in the park to hold us over until a late dinner. Sometimes Dad met us there and drove us home.

Randall's Island was a very special place to us. When I was young the family gathered there for picnics. Sometimes my mother and my aunt walked us across the bridge, a trip made interesting by the two observation towers overlooking The Bronx Kill. This was a favorite part of the walk; my cousins and I often pretended to be pirates or knights. Randall's Island was usually empty during the week. Many evenings my father drove us there to escape the heat. On the weekends he liked to park beneath the Triborough Bridge where he washed and waxed his car while I played nearby. The broad fields were great places to fly a kite or to launch my moon rocket or to play catch. Sometimes marching bands practiced in the parking lot. We counted the cars of long freight trains on the Hell Gate Railroad Bridge. A stone bridge connected Randall's Island to Ward's Island, which housed the Manhattan Psychiatric Hospital. Cars had to stop at the guard booth before crossing.

The shores of Randall's Island were lined with huge rectangular stones; from them one had a good view of Manhattan. The island had a marina for the harbor police, and a police station as well. There was a large playground with a wading pool, basketball hoops, and horseshoe stakes. Mom liked to talk to the park attendant, an old black woman in a white uniform; her name was Billie. She liked me because we had the same first name. She often turned on the sprinklers for me even when I was the only child in the playground. Sometimes my father brought along my bike; I liked to ride the asphalt path around Downing Stadium.

Being in Randall's Island was like being in the country; I could see the sky and the water and all seemed surrounded by mystery:

the Little Hell Gate, The Bronx Kill, the psychiatric hospital. The pillars of the Triborough and especially of the Hell Gate Bridges were tall and broad—all in all, enormous—and standing beneath them filled me with awe. Except for those which lined the walks, there were not many trees, but there were a couple of willows near the western shore that were good for climbing. There were bushes near the stadium where we hunted fireflies and other insects to feed my pet frog. When my parakeets died we buried them beneath a certain fence post near our usual parking spot. This special place of wonder and freedom was just a mile or two from home.

Saint Mary's Park was also nearby and provided a variety of entertainment. On a full outing, my mom and my aunt took us to the main playground, which offered many swings, monkey bars, and a wading pool. For a shorter trip, we might go just as far as the playground near the southwest entrance, or play in the fields near Saint Ann's Avenue. There were rocks to climb, and one winter evening I found a washing machine cover and sledded down Dead Man's Hill, which was at the northern end of the park. Walking to the park we passed Saint Ann's Church. The old gravestones were fascinating, as was the cannon which pointed out from the churchyard. Saint Francis and Saint Joseph's Hospitals were near the park; they seemed surrounded by an aura of silence.

We also made summer trips to The Bronx Zoo. Mom packed a lunch and we took the bus up Southern Boulevard. We entered at the south entrance and worked our way north. Our first stop was a pond where we could see ducks and geese. We made our way to the African Plains, then crossed a wooden bridge over the lions and tigers. By the time we got to the sea lions, I was always hot and tired; I envied their ability to swim gracefully in the cool water.

In those days the public could feed the animals. For a quarter one could purchase fish from a machine to throw to the seals. We bought marshmallows and bread to toss at the elephants. They were fed all day long, by hundreds of kids. In one of the houses there was a mandrill who seemed to hate women; when one got close to his cage, he put his face up to the glass and snarled ferociously. Once a tiger backed up to the bars of its cage and urinated on my surprised cousin; we did not sit near him on the bus ride home. At the north end of the park was a pond with an island; we called it Monkey Island because a family of monkeys lived on it. A pair of swans often swam there. After the exhibits closed Mom and I sat on the benches near Southern Boulevard and fed the squirrels.

My mother liked to walk, and she knew the neighborhood quite well. Sometimes we walked past the old Lincoln Hospital to Ward's bakery; day-old goods were sold at a discount. The treats made it worth it. Walks to the Mott Haven Library were occasionally made longer by a diversion to the Safeway supermarket, which was a few blocks farther. Several times the family walked over the Willis Avenue Bridge to the Feast of Our Lady of Mount Carmel in East Harlem. The streets were crowded; there was a band in the park, and on the way home we stopped at Patsy's for pizza. Another annual event was Saint Jude's Bazaar, held at a church in upper Manhattan; fortunately we did not walk to that one, but we did stroll across the University Heights Bridge to the taxi stand at the Major Deegan.

As crime increased in the 1960s, our walking excursions decreased. By the end of the decade, walks to The Hub revealed more and more condemned or burned-out buildings. Several blocks between Brook and Saint Ann's Avenues were condemned; eventually they were razed and left as empty lots. Rumor had it that a new Lincoln Hospital was to be constructed on the site, but that did not happen; the lots remained empty, and eventually vegetation grew amid the debris. We stopped going to Saint Mary's Park to play, though we did walk there to see the spot where a small airplane had crashed.

As we grew older our mothers allowed us to play without their immediate presence; in other words, we could go downstairs by ourselves to play as they watched us from the window. We had to stay in sight, at our end of the block, and not around the corner. If we wanted money for a soda or ice cream, Mom wrapped it in some paper and threw it down. The street was always busy with traffic; at rush hour it swarmed with commuters emerging from the subway. This was not a good set up for stickball, but we did play a lot of punchball and touch football, using sidewalk cracks and manhole covers as yard markers or bases. We also played Johnny-on-the-pony, ringolevio, red-light-green-light, skelly (sidewalk checkers), tag, hot-beans-and-butter (tag played with a belt—I was not a fast runner and did not participate) and other games that we invented.

Grant's sometimes put out very large boxes for the trash. We took them, cut off the ends, got inside and crawled down the street trying to "steamroller" the other kids. The game was so much fun that it usually did not end until the box was destroyed. Inspired by the comic books, we played Batman and Robin. Two big kids were the heroes and several little ones the villains. When one side caught the other, a pretend rumble began.

Skelly, also called skully or sidewalk checkers, was a favorite pastime. A pattern of boxes was drawn and the object of the game was to shoot a bottle cap from box one through box thirteen, and, sometimes, back to one again. Boxes one through four were at each corner of the pavement slab; boxes five through twelve were in pairs midway along the four sides of the square; box thirteen was in dead center of the square; it was surrounded by a larger box known as "dead man's land." If a player's piece wound up here, it was "dead"; a reward of boxes was offered to any other player who knocked the trapped piece out with his or her own. Players could use their own turn to move forward to the next box either by landing their piece completely in it or by hitting their piece into another player's, knocking it into or out of dead-man's land or blasting it far off the playing area. A player's turn ended when he or she failed to advance to the next box.

There was a slab of concrete outside 514 which was very smooth and made for a great game. Most of us made our checkers by filling bottle caps with melted crayons, though a few talented kids learned to patiently scrape the lip of a soda or beer bottle over the curb; if done just right, the lip came off as one piece and could be used for skelly. But if another player hit one of these glass pieces hard enough, it would shatter. We spent hours crawling around the sidewalk, wearing the knees off our jeans. One day as I was working on shooting my cap into box three I heard a strange noise overhead. I looked up to see a cat falling; it landed just a few feet from me. It slowly stood up and staggered off. I was amazed; I never knew cats could survive such falls.

In addition to our own games, there were traveling rides which visited the block. One was called the Blue Moon or the Half Moon; kids sat on benches while the contraption rocked back and forth. On another, standing children lined a metal cage that spun around. Yet another was a small Ferris wheel. Vendors selling Italian ices or ice cream wandered by; they were eventually replaced by merchants of snow cones: crushed ice with flavoring. Some carts sold oranges; the orange was put on a spinning peeler which removed the skin in one long curly strip; it was fascinating to watch when nothing else was going on. Sometimes neighborhood kids got milk boxes and sold old comic books; this was my favorite kind of shopping.

Every few weeks we varied the toys we played with, following the neighborhood fad of the moment. Roller-skating might be in for a week, then bicycles came out. Scooters made of milk boxes, two-by-fours, and old skate wheels were always impressive. We cycled through water pistols, cowboy guns, army toys, marbles, tops, yo-yos, baseball cards, super balls, water balloons, punchball, and football. Given the consumerism of the 1950s and 1960s, all sorts of toys became available. Two of my prize guns were a black-handled cowboy gun which made a twang after it was fired, and a bazooka which shot plastic rockets.

Dad and I tried our hands at flying a gas-powered model airplane, but we were not that good at piloting; however, we had better luck launching our chemically-propelled moon rocket. Model railroading was popular, and several times my father took me downtown to see the Lionel's Christmas display. By the time I entered junior high, trains were out and electric racing cars were in. Various toys and games moved in and out of my life: Lincoln Logs, Colorforms, Monopoly, Careers, Fort Apache, Silly Putty, Play-Doh, Robert the Robot, View Master, Erector Sets, Battle Cry, and Magic Rocks are some names that I remember. Some of the games like Mousetrap and Operation were advertised on television, but I did not get them until I myself became a parent.

We were the first television generation, and my parents were the first in their family to get a television. Their apartment was quite popular for a while, but eventually everyone bought televisions of their own. I grew up with *Romper Room, Captain Kangaroo, Freddie the Fireman, The Sandy Becker Show, The Mickey Mouse Club*, and all sorts of cartoons. There was *Combat, The Rifleman, Paladin, Branded, My Favorite Martian, Car 54,* and *Bonanza*. There was an abundance of movies, with the *Early Show* at dinner time, and *The Late Show* and *The Late Late Show* at night, and there seemed to be a good number of Yankees games to watch on WPIX. When I started at DeWitt Clinton as a sophomore, I was on the second shift; it was fashionable to stay up late, watch Johnny Carson, and talk about the show at lunch.

I had my own pocket transistor radio; as I got older I spent many hours cruising the AM dial. My mom was a WMCA Good Guys fan, and especially loved Jack and Benny. But at night I ventured off to WABC; it had Cousin Brucie and commercials from Dennison's the Men's Clothier—"money talks and nobody walks." It was a thrill to get my first FM radio. Thirty years later, I still have it; though the tuning knob fell off and I have to put a finger inside the resulting hole to change the station, it still plays, and I still remember my fascination with WNEW FM: Scott Muni, Alison Steele—what greats.

I listened to plenty of Yankees games, but when I became old enough to understand the sport, the Yankees began to do quite poorly. The first ball game I attended was at the Polo Grounds: the Mets played the Cardinals. I went to a few games at Shea Stadium, and once got to see Willie Mays, who was a Met at the time, hit a home run simultaneously with a thunderbolt. But we were Yankees fans and only went to Shea if we got free tickets, which my father sometimes did. I was lucky to see some of the great Yankees stars of the '60s before they retired: Richardson, Kubek, Boyer, Mantle, Maris, Howard. My mother was an avid Yankees fan who loved to remember the great teams of the past; she really knew how to root and she made the games fun. Even when the Yankees were losing, the stadium had an aura to it—it was a thrill just to be there. Almost every time I passed by it on the Woodlawn train, I peered through the window to catch a brief view of the playing field.

Summer would not be summer without baseball and the Fourth of July. As July approached there was a gradual increase in noise as various kids tried out their fireworks. I was not allowed to play with firecrackers myself; but my parents permitted a few snakes, snaps, and sparklers. Other kids were more reckless. Various and risky experiments were made. Beer cans were halved and reassembled with a firecracker inside; the top half of the can was launched in the air. Larger fireworks brought more spectacular and dangerous results. I saw garbage can covers blown five stories in the air, and a manhole cover lifted about fifteen feet. At night on the Fourth there often was a fireworks war between the two sides of the street; by morning the street was littered with paper. Usually the Fourth was a time to stay home, close the windows, calm the dog, and hope that nobody's apartment would be set on fire by a stray rocket. It was quite noisy, and, since fireworks were thrown from the roofs, it was not safe to walk in the streets.

Halloween had become a time to dress up and go trick-or-treating, something which was not practiced when my mother was young, though she talked of a ragamuffin parade on Thanksgiving. Mom did not let us knock on strangers' doors, but she did take us to our aunts' apartments. We could stand out by the subway and trick-or-treat the emerging commuters. Sometimes people threw pennies which we chased and gathered on the dark sidewalk. A favorite Halloween game was to put chalk in a sock and hit each other.

Thanksgiving involved much eating. My mother spent hours preparing the meal. We always had turkey and lasagna. Preparation for the lasagna began with trips to East Harlem, Tremont Avenue, or Arthur Avenue. Noodles, ricotta cheese, and mozzarella were purchased at various stores. Mom often cooked two turkeys, put one in her shopping cart, and wheeled it up to my paternal grandparents who lived at 141st and Cypress. On the way back we might stop at my aunt's for coffee and desert.

As Christmas approached, my dad began assembling the Lionel trains. He put a plywood board over the dining room table, laid track, and assembled a Plasticville city. Dad worked on Wall Street, and he often shopped at the discount stores that were in the vicinity of the present World Trade Center. He accumulated all sorts of contraptions at bargain prices: revolving radar and floodlights, a microphone that told the trains to stop and go, milk and log loading platforms, all of which provided hours of amusement. Over the years the layout grew; it expanded to include a nearby buffet that my mom connected to the main layout by making mountains out of painted shopping bags.

There were plenty of relatives to visit on Christmas, and I never could escape the family's day-after-Christmas trip to the Hub for the clearance sales. My parents had a white tree which had to be renewed with a spray of snow—I think it contained fiberglass; it certainly made our forearms red and itchy. One of my aunts had a tree made of aluminum; lights could not be placed on it; rather, a light projector with a rotating color panel was aimed at it to make red, yellow, and blue patterns.

On New Year's Eve we gathered and watched Guy Lombardo. At midnight we ate herring and held coins in our hands. To the children the night seemed to go on forever; once we had our fill of soda and treats, it became a struggle to stay awake.

The long nights, school, and homework did not allow for much outside play during the winters, at least not during the week. As I grew older the city did not seem to receive many big snowstorms, but there were a few that provided enough snow to allow us to build forts and to have snowball wars. Sometimes we fought the kids across the street, but it was a wide street, and only the older kids were strong enough to throw a snowball to the other side.

My most vivid memories of winter were of the times when there was no heat or hot water. I learned to bundle myself completely under the blankets; my breath eventually heated up the space and helped keep me warm. Getting out of bed in the morning was a chore. Not having hot water was the worst—a warm shower at least took the chill out of the bones. If the situation went on too long, we might boil enough water to partly fill up the bathtub. Sometimes I might visit my aunt's apartment and take a warm bath there. We had an exchange program, so sometimes my cousin put her coat over her pajamas and stopped at our house for a shower. When I played at a church gym, I could shower there. My mother was fairly stoic about the whole affair; she grew up in a cold-water flat on 134th Street. My parents were somewhat shocked when I decided to move to Wisconsin; I told them over and over that I have never been so warm—here, the cold is outside, where it belongs.

The apartment we lived in was quite nice; it had six rooms, and it was not a railroad flat. (My father's parents had a railroad flat. One had to pass through the bedrooms to walk across the apartment, and there were two front doors: one in the front room and one in the dining room.) My parents' apartment had two small bedrooms off the living room, all of which overlooked 138th Street. French doors separated the dining room from the living room, and there was a small unheated bedroom off the dining room. A hall exited the dining room, passed by the kitchen and bathroom, and ended in the outside door. Midnight trips to the bathroom were scary; I had to walk through the entire apartment and take down the bar of the "police lock" that braced the front door but blocked the door to the bathroom. I often listened for noise in the hallway before I did this—I did not want to let the bogeyman in. The tenements had dumbwaiters which were nailed shut—our uncles told us that was where the bogeyman lived.

The back rooms looked out onto a big air shaft. Clotheslines ran from side to side, and, as one of my aunts lived next door, but in the next building, she and my mom often hung out the laundry at the same time so they could chat. When I was very young, an accordion player sometimes walked through the air shafts and collected the coins people threw down. I believe there was once an organ grinder with a monkey. As crime increased these basement routes became more dangerous, and the only music we got came from blasting stereos.

There was a cockfighting ring in a nearby basement, and the roosters did crow at dawn. When the police raided it, they closed off the entire street. It all took quite a while; the police wagons had to make several trips. I counted seventy-eight people hauled off, and I had not seen the beginning of the raid. It was quite an event. Some of those being arrested waved at the crowd, enjoying their moment of fame. There were women and children and people with picnic baskets. Even the roosters were apprehended.

I grew up in the time between the old Bronx and the new. In early memories, coal trucks still made deliveries; the burnt ashes were put out in barrels or used to cover the winter ice. A rag collector still made the rounds in a horse cart. A Scottish funeral procession featured a horse-drawn hearse and bagpipes. A street sweeper had a large broom and a barrel on wheels. Brook Avenue was lined with paving stones; the trolley tracks were still visible on St. Ann's Avenue. Stores stayed open past dark, and their lights illuminated the night. Taxicabs did not refuse one's service. We might take an evening trip to Jahn's or to an Italian restaurant on Melrose Avenue.

The riots that occurred during two summers in the mid-1960s marked a great change. Stores began to close earlier, and the windows were covered with steel roll-down gates, giving the neighborhood a gloomy, fortressed, appearance. According to my memory, and to neighborhood gossip, both of which may not be too reliable, the first summer's riots were triggered by a boxing match between a Cuban and a Puerto Rican. Because the other fighter left the ring too early, the Cuban won even though he had been knocked out. An unhappy crowd gathered outside the Puerto Rico Theater, which happened to be hosting a Cuban musical group. The crowd grew throughout the late afternoon, and by about five o'clock disturbances broke out.

Rioting in a subsequent summer followed disturbances in other areas. Many of the local residents sat by their windows to watch the activities. As a main thoroughfare 138th Street was a gathering spot both for rioters and for the police. One night I watched as city buses and rental trucks unloaded an army of officers. The strategy seemed to be to drive the rioters into the side streets. After the first night the police arrived early to try to prevent crowds from gathering. Sometimes crowds formed on the side streets and swelled their way onto ours. Eventually they wore themselves out. We took care to get home well before sundown. It was a sad time.

But there were noble times as well. People in the neighborhood, both old-timers and newcomers, watched out for each other. On a chilly fall evening an orderly crowd gathered west of Willis Avenue to glimpse the Pope on his way to Yankee Stadium. During the first blackout, there were no disturbances. Everyone seemed to help others find their way. I was playing football with a friend; he threw the ball to me and the lights went out. All the lights went out. After our initial amazement we had to find the football. The tenement staircases were hard to navigate in the utter darkness, even for those who knew them well. But people helped each other and shared what light they had. It was quite an evening.

One of the remnants of the old Bronx was the family shoeshine parlor. It was built in an age when decorum was important; indeed, the architecture of the neighborhood showed an appreciation of style. Many of the tenements were trimmed with ornate modillions; hallways had inlaid tiles with decorative patterns; moldings trimmed living rooms and bedrooms, and even the bathtub had clawed legs. The housing projects of the post-World War II era were bland and functional. The architecture of the shoeshine parlor in which I worked, covered as it was by fifty years of enamel paint, showed a love for detail and craft. A shoeshine parlor is a wooden structure built onto the side of a tenement. Though we affectionately referred to ours as the Shanty, it was by no means crudely built. Its facade consisted of wood strips carefully joined together into rectangular panels surmounted by smaller wooden rectangles which added support and decoration. These panels were trimmed with molding. The front had two sliding doors; the south side had a regular door with a skeleton key lock, and the north side abutted the subway entrance. There were six large windows, four on the front, and one on each of the sides; all of these were topped by transoms. Awnings provided shade. The interior featured a marble stand on which stood a bench of green leather trimmed with dark wood. There were storage areas under the bench. The lower section of the marble supported brass footrests. By the time I worked there, the ends of the footrests were worn sharp from the movement of thousands of feet and were covered with electrical tape to prevent us from cutting our hands on them. There was a gas radiator on one side of the stand, and a cabinet topped by an ornate National Cash Register on the other.

Uncle Al, who owned the place when I was growing up, worked the side by the cash register. His fingers had worn out certain keys—25¢ was no longer visible—and had soiled the edges of others with polish. His oldest worker had the side by the subway station; he got to sit on the open window in between shines, and to carve his initials in the layers of paint which covered the railing. The youngest worked in the middle and had to move every time a customer came or left, getting a cold draft on a sweaty back every time the door opened during the winter. Shoeshine parlors dotted the neighborhood. There was one on 139th street off Brook Avenue, one on 138th and Cypress, and two on Saint Ann's Avenue, although one sold newspapers and candy. So many shoeshine parlors in such a small area suggested a time when shoes were important. They were made to last, and they needed to be cared for. But America was changing; goods were becoming disposable. I entered the business during its decline. The 1960s saw the advent of vinyl shoes, the rise of sneakers and sandals, and a general disregard for formality. The Shanty, which used to be open every day, was reduced to being open only on Fridays and weekends. Customers dwindled and our prices went up.

Shining shoes was a great job. When it was crowded, we hustled, and it was a physical exertion to keep up with the pace: we did not want to lose any customers to the kids with their shoeshine boxes who sometimes waited across the street by the subway exit. When it rained we played rummy for nickels. Saturdays were tough: a twelve-hour day; as a young teenager, it gave me a sense of accomplishment to make it through. In the summers we were soaked with sweat, and we drank water from old mayonnaise jars to keep us going.

I began working in the Shanty when I was about eleven. For the first few months I was an apprentice: I got to wash the shoes and someone else finished the job. After washing enough shoes to show that I would not soil the customers' socks, and after providing enough free shines to various friends and relatives, I was eventually allowed to do a complete shine on a complete stranger.

The shine began with a wash which was applied with a round brush and removed with a wash rag; this was followed by applying and removing two coats of polish; the finale was to apply a small amount of silicone cream and to buff the shoe with a shine rag. Complicated jobs such as shoes with white threads, dye jobs, and two-tone boots were not immediately given to me, but I eventually worked my way into them. The whole shine took about two or three minutes. The secret to a bootblack's success was a quality brush; each worker had his own pair, and when we received a dollar for a quarter shine, we carved a notch in the handle. I enjoyed it all: the physical work, the joy of taking something old and renewing it, the pride of earning my own money. I liked conversations with the customers, and it was fun to watch the world go by from our wonderful windows. Though the Shanty was unharmed by the riots, it had been the victim of a break-in, so it was decided to replace the large windows with plywood panels that had plexiglass portholes—an era had ended.

Uncle Al was very nice to us. Most of his workers were nephews or family friends, and Al seemed to delight in treating the boys to fun. On Saturdays, he often took us out for dinner; on Sundays, we might make a brief visit to the pool hall on 137th Street. During the summer, he often took us swimming at Palisades. Al picked us up after finishing his night job. We stopped at an Italian deli, purchased some sandwiches, and were off. Al loved to swim, and we spent the morning in the deep end of the pool. There were few people in that section, just a few divers and one or two old men doing laps. We liked to hold onto the ledge of the waterfall and to remain there for long periods while the water cascaded over our heads and shoulders. The salt water never burned the eyes. Lunch lasted as long as it took Al to eat a sandwich and to smoke a cigar. We stayed at the pool until early afternoon, then it was back to The Bronx so that Al could get some sleep before working the midnight shift at the Railway Express Agency.

I stopped working in the shoeshine parlor in 1971. By then we had moved to the Fordham Road area, and I had another job in Manhattan working as a stock clerk for an office in a church. Living near Fordham Road offered new excitement. I could walk to school again, something I had not been able to do since third grade. I could walk to Jahn's, take a date to Steak and Brew, and return to the Fordham campus at night to swim or to study. I took long jogs exploring new neighborhoods and the park along The Bronx River. I could visit the campus bar, the Pennywhistle, and dance at the Pick and Shovel. I could hang out at "Scratch Park" on Webster Avenue with my friends until sunrise. In summer I could just sit on the Rose Hill campus and read a book—a pastoral life just a few yards from Fordham Road. There were occasional dances in the campus center, and at one I met a lovely woman, a Lehman College student, who had grown up on 141st Street just off Willis Avenue. Her family had moved to the East Village, so our courtship involved long subway rides. After I graduated, we married and set up a new life in Madison, Wisconsin.

Given these new attractions, I did not miss the South Bronx as much then as I do now. I think back on those summers which my mother filled with fun; on the times my father took me fishing at Ferry Point or for walks in Saint Mary's Park; on Uncle Al with his wonderful spirit of life and his sense of fun; on my cousins and friends and the childhood games we played; and on my aunts, with their treats and conversations and sense of family. It was the only childhood I could have, and I have never outgrown it.

Fordham

I grew up in the South Bronx. 138th Street. There was not much Bronx south of us: the Millbrook Projects, the Major Deegan, Bruckner Boulevard, and the railroad yard. As reflected in the first two letters of our phone number: MO, we lived in the Mott Haven section of The Bronx. Childhood in the fifties and early sixties consisted of school, homework, black-and-white television, and playing on the street with cousins and friends. But during the mid-1960s, the innocence of my childhood world seemed to fade.

Eventually, after a couple of riots and an increase in crime, the neighborhood took on an aura of gloom. Stores closed early and were protected by steel roll-down gates. The dismal effect was most apparent on Sundays, when most of the stores were closed, and the nights seemed a bit darker without the extra light from shop windows. The side streets were blighted by tenements abandoned due to arson or condemnation. The city razed several blocks between Brook and Saint Ann's Avenues. According to local gossip, a new Lincoln Hospital would be built there. It was not. Eventually vegetation began to grow amid the rubble.

In a spectacular fire, PS 9 burned down; the site became an asphalt playground. In another spectacular fire, the tenement just east of Saint Luke's Church caught fire. Despite being right across the street from the fire station, the top two stories of the building were quickly and completely engulfed in flame, so I always suspected that the fire was no accident. Although it was night, everyone gathered outside to watch. It was the first time I saw a hook and ladder in action: the fireman at the top sprayed a strong jet of water through the black, then white, clouds of smoke which reflected the orange flames. The firefighters were the true working-class heroes; they risked their lives to save lives in a neighborhood plagued by arson and false alarms.

Neighbors moved. For years, it seemed, my parents talked about moving. They did not appear to be in a great hurry to do so: we had plenty of relatives in the neighborhood, and we were paying less than forty dollars a month for our six-room rent-controlled apartment. So they could afford to be fussy. Long Island was out. Dad worked on Wall Street, and the subway was a quick and convenient ride to work. We looked at a small house off Bruckner Boulevard. My parents came of age during the Depression; I suspect that down payments and mortgages were alien to them. Sometimes we drove the Grand Concourse and saw signs for apartments; most were brokered by agents who required a fee. My parents were somewhat frugal: to see the Statue of Liberty, we took the Staten Island Ferry and looked at it in passing; to see the Empire State Building, we went to 34th Street and looked up; they were not going to pay for an elevator ride. And no, I never went to Freedomland. Our apartment-seeking trips up the Concourse were fruitless; however, we did discover a great pizza parlor at 184th Street. There was always money for pizza.

Though I continued to live on 138th street, I began to drift away from it. School kept me busy. In fourth grade, I was put in an academically advanced program, which meant commuting to school: PS 31 on 144th and the Concourse, then JHS 145 on Clay and 165th, then JHS 117 on 175th. High school brought an even longer commute to DeWitt Clinton. I had no school friends in the immediate neighborhood. But a kid who lived across the hall was in the Boy Scouts, and when I was eleven, I joined his troop; it met at a church on 76th and Lexington in Manhattan. Eventually, I got a job at the church. It was a fifteen-minute subway ride, and Mom seemed glad that I was able to get out of the neighborhood. I made new friends on the Upper East Side, and I enjoyed hanging out there. I did have to check in by phone—it only cost a dime—and I had to be back by ten, or eventually eleven, but I had a lot more freedom than I would have had in the South Bronx, where Mom did not even want me to go around the corner.

Going away to college was something I really had not thought about too much. I was young: a sixteen-year-old high-school senior who would not turn seventeen until several weeks into his first semester of college. Room and board would be an additional expense. New York had an abundance of colleges and a fine transportation system. Going to college certainly was something my parents expected of me. I worked hard in high school to get good grades. I bought review books and took practice Regents exams and SAT tests. My parents valued "getting an education." My father dropped out of high school twice: during the Depression he had to work to help out his family; during the sixties, he left the GED program because his job needed him to work overtime. My mother was the only one of her siblings to complete high school. I was one of the first in the family to attend college.

There was no thought of college tours: I had applied to Fordham and we knew where the campus was; we had passed it on many return trips from the Bronx Zoo, and we knew how to get there by subway and bus. What else was there to know? I simply showed up on the first day, got a brief orientation, talked to a guy I vaguely knew who had also attended Clinton, saw a concert by Tina Turner (who no longer was with Ike), and I was a college freshman. Scholarships paid for about half of the tuition, and Dad and I split the rest. I could live at home, which I am sure made my parents happy. I loved the Fordham campus: the hubbub of the city seemed to disappear amid its green lawns and trees. The students were nice; most of them were commuters, but the Campus Center offered the opportunity to meet and make friends.

Only years later did I come to realize what a great fit Fordham was for a young student such as myself whose family did not know much about the college experience: classes were small, and the teachers were very accessible. Their help and encouragement were much appreciated. At the time, Fordham, in partnership with Columbia University, offered a five-year program in which I could earn a BA in English and a BS in Engineering. That seemed interesting to me, and would help me defer any final decisions about what to do with my life. So I began college with courses in the liberal arts, physics, and calculus. I made friends in my calculus class and learned that if I walked up Willis Avenue I could arrive at the Third Avenue El at the same time as they did on their commute from Manhattan and Queens. The El went through the heart of The Bronx, and I remember the fresh morning sun illuminating the ruined tenements. The El did not seem to run as frequently at night. Once my buddies and I decided to take the El as the first leg of our trip to one of the Schaeffer music concerts in Central Park. It took so long for the train to come that we missed almost the entire show. I think we got there for the last song.

I remember my first college dance, a huge mixer in the Campus Center. I had taken the Woodlawn train and was waiting at the corner of Fordham and Jerome for the crosstown bus. Soon a bus pulled up and its front door opened. This was not a city bus; it was a charter packed with young women. The driver asked if I knew how to get to Fordham University. I said I did, and that I was going there. There was a little space up front, and I stood next to the driver and navigated him along Fordham Road. If only the guys from Clinton (which was not co-ed at the time) could have seen me! The Fordham student body was primarily male, so women from other colleges were bused in for the mixers. I could dance with them, but without a car I would probably never see them again. Nevertheless, it was a memorable night: I got a free bus ride, and, at the young age of sixteen, I managed to sneak into my first college dance.

Near the end of my first semester, I made a decision that would shape the rest of my life: I decided to become an English major. I earned good grades in my pre-engineering classes, but they were just not fun. So on a gray December day, I walked up to the appropriate office and declared my major. English. Just English. No more five-year program. No Columbia University.

And my parents made a life-changing decision as well: We were moving! To an apartment on Morris Avenue, just a half a block south of Fordham Road. Second floor, front. A cousin lived in the building, fifth floor rear, and he was supposed to get the apartment, but his furniture did not fit, so he offered it to my aunt, who decided that she did not want to leave the South Bronx. When we were told about the apartment, Dad thought it would be a good idea to take it. There was some initial difficulty with the landlord, which I suspect was due to our Hispanic surname, but after some background checks, we were in. We could not believe it. I would be able to walk to college. The IRT and IND stations were nearby, so commuting to Manhattan would be easy. Fordham Road was the shopping center of The Bronx. There were restaurants, movie theaters, and stores of all sorts; Mom could walk to Alexander's in a matter of minutes.

It took a few weeks to get the apartment ready. When my classes were done for the day, I met up with Mom, then we spent the rest of the afternoon plastering and painting. Mom was quite handy and had a lot of experience in these areas. The apartment looked out on Morris Avenue, a long street of northbound, one-way traffic. To the south, Bronx Community College was on the corner of 184th Street; to the north, Woolworth's was across the intersection at Fordham Road. Our building was on the west side of the street, which had three large apartment buildings, a row of four private houses, a small liquor store, and the entrance to Monroe Business College. Merit Chicken was on the corner at Fordham Road.

The bedrooms were large. Mine seemed to be three times the size of my previous one. There was ample room for my bookcases, desk, typewriter, and stereo. I was a teenager with a room to decorate; it was the beginning of the 1970s, and I indulged my fancy. I chose a very dark blue paint for the walls. I bought a fixture, taped the wires onto an electric cord, and popped in a black light. Black light posters were popular, and I bought a few. Fluorescent tempera paint was available, and I had spent a number of hours tracing the inside of the Sgt. Pepper album. The four Beatles in their colorful regalia made an awesome black-light poster. I painted my bookcases flat black and trimmed them in fluorescent red. George Harrison's solo album included a poster of him in a dark outfit that faded into darkness at the bottom. With two such posters, I could invert one and completely cover the inside of my bedroom door. It took a bit of begging, but one of my college friends gave me hers, and I was delighted. My room was an obvious masterpiece which I wanted to complete by painting the ceiling black and decorating it with fluorescent stars; my father, however, would not let me, and I did not push the issue.

The rest of the apartment was decorated in a more traditional manner. My mother had a large collection of knickknacks, and my father had a collection of hardcover novels. The books were relegated to two short book cases in the living room; the knickknacks filled a china closet, the top shelves of the bookcases, and two additional shelves that were mounted on the wall. In the days before cable television and computers, hobbies were popular. Included among the collection of gimcrackery were works of sand art: the kit contained a glass goblet, colored sand, and directions; somehow, the layers of sand created a desert scene. The walls had a few paint-by-number paintings and plaques made by gluing gold string and colored gravel to form figures of matadors. The top of my wardrobe was the display for plastic models. I still have three of the Aurora figurines my father so carefully assembled and patiently painted: a Native American chief, woman, and warrior. Of the many models I put together, my masterpiece was a gladiator with the broken shield and severed arm of his opponent at his feet. Unlike the airplanes, ships, cars, and knights, this figure had a lot of detail that needed to be painted in, and I somehow managed to do it.

The living room featured other treasures. The sofa and chair were purchased after my parents won the jackpot at a Castle Hill bingo parlor. The Chinese-figurine lamps and the sunburst clock were won at Palisades Amusement Park. My contribution was an AM/FM table radio that I won at a PS 43 fund-raiser. My parents loved to shop, and after years of not buying new furnishings because "we were going to move," we now splurged. We bought a new kitchen set, linoleum tiling for the kitchen floor, and carpeting for the living room and bedrooms. The apartment was tidy and warm; we were happy to settle in.

Fordham Road was indeed a shopper's paradise. From University Avenue in the west, extending almost to Southern Boulevard in the east, Fordham Road was lined with stores. There were bakeries, restaurants, jewelers, pizzerias, record stores, clothing stores—you name it! Grocery stores were numerous. There were A&Ps at Valentine Avenue, University Avenue, 184th and Jerome, and 183rd and Jerome. Bohack was one block off the Concourse near Union Hospital at Ryre Avenue and 187th, and also under the El on Jerome Avenue; Associated was at 183rd and Morris; Daitch was at the corner of Fordham Road and Davidson Avenue. At least that is how Mom remembered it. As a teenager I did not pay much attention to grocery stores. But Mom studied the supermarket ads in the Daily News; she followed the sales and price fluctuations as others might follow the stock market. We ate well.

There were several five-and-tens in the area: Grant's was just around the corner at Fordham Road, between Morris and Walton Avenues, and Woolworth's was across the street from it. East of the Grand Concourse were S. S. Kresge and another Woolworth's. There were men's and women's clothing stores: Messenger's was at the triangular corner of 188th and Fordham; Loehmann's at Jerome; Wallach's was by Tiebot Avenue; Bond's was near Valentine Avenue, so was Lerner's. Shoe stores included Florsheim, Adler, Tom McAn, Wise, Miles, and Beck's. Again, that is according to Mom's memory. To me, most of these stores were a blur. I was more interested in the Jahn's Ice Cream Parlor and the newly-opened Steak and Brew.

The crown jewel of Fordham Road, the ultimate place to shop, of course was Alexander's. My parents were great fans of Alexander's. When we lived on 138th Street, we made frequent walks to the Hub. I worked on 76th Street, and after I got paid on Saturdays, I often walked down to the 59th Street store to buy records. My father drove us to Rego Park, White Plains, and even to Milford, Connecticut. I think we had visited almost every Alexander's in existence at that time. But now we were just a few blocks from what seemed to be the best of the chain. The Fordham Alexander's had it all, and at a good price. From the top floor, which had toys, hobbies, and linens, to the basement, which had men's clothes, a record shop, and inexpensive shoes, the store was full of bargains and eager shoppers. My primary interests were record albums and jeans. I bought a Nehru jacket that I thought looked pretty good on me. I think I paid ten dollars for it. I still have it; I wish it still fit.

My mother was interested in almost every good bargain. Mom wound up living on Morris Avenue for thirty-two years, and Alexander's was her exercise and her hobby. She got to know the ladies who worked there, and they often told her when sales were coming. A lot of the merchandise was displayed on tables that had drawers where extra goods were stored. If you did not find the right size shoes on the discount table, you opened the drawer and continued the search. Sometimes Mom reserved an item by taking it to another area and putting it in a drawer where it did not belong. When it went on sale, she retrieved it and purchased it at a discount.

My father's brother, who had worked in the Garment District, claimed that the same suits were delivered to Alexander's as to other more expensive clothing stores. My mother learned that not only could you get a good buy on suits at Alexander's, but you could get an even better buy if you purchased them one piece at a time. The jacket might come in on clearance, and, a few weeks later, the pants. On occasion, the matching vest might appear as well. Mom was quite skilled with the sewing machine, so she could tailor the pants herself. My father accumulated quite a wardrobe. Indeed, there was no shortage of clothes in our household. My parents had lived through the Depression, and I think that it was a great comfort to them to be able to afford a bit of abundance. Especially if it came at a good price.

In addition to the large red letters that spelled ALEXANDER'S, the Fordham skyline was dominated by the tower of the Dollar Savings Bank. The interior of this magnificent art-deco building seemed palatial; the enormous windows and chandeliers illuminated its elegance. The walls of the banking area rose several stories, and the east wall had murals. The center of the banking area had tellers' stations trimmed with brass bars. Eventually plexiglass was installed. The clock tower was a valuable asset to me, as I could always check the time when I went to or from the Fordham campus.

During my first year on Morris Avenue, I actually spent a lot of time in Manhattan. I worked on 76th Street and had friends there. As I made friends at Fordham, I spent more time on campus. The gym had a swimming pool that I enjoyed, and there was a running track next to the campus center. There were movies, dances in the Rathskeller, and concerts in the gym. Though I was not much of a sports fan at the time, I did go to a basketball game the season that Digger Phelps was coach. To me, the campus was a bit of country in The Bronx, and I enjoyed sitting on the lawn outside the old library, reading a book, or trying to get a suntan.

Across the street from the campus, on Webster Avenue, was the Pennywhistle, a bar frequented by many of Fordham's young scholars. A few doors north, a dance club called the Pick and Shovel offered live music or disk jockeys and was quite crowded on weekends. Tony's Delicatessen opened, and it became possible to buy salads and cold cuts. Just across from the Pennywhistle was Rose Hill Park, which we called Scratch Park, because, as someone said, it was just a little scratch of asphalt beside the railroad tracks. My friends and I often spent many hours there at night. It was a place to meet before going to the Pennywhistle, and a place to hang out after closing time.

The easiest way to get from campus to these Webster Avenue attractions was to walk a well-beaten path that led down an incline and beneath the Third Avenue El. There was a fence bordering the Fordham railroad station. The iron bars had been pried apart, presumably by some alumni wanting to leave a gift for the future student body. There was enough space to wiggle through sideways while carefully establishing a footing on the staircase. The rest was easy: ascend the stairs, cross the passenger bridge over the railroad tracks, and descend onto Webster Avenue, conveniently just across from the Pennywhistle. So many of us took this route that the university had constructed a guard post at the beginning of the path where an IBI patrolman watched our comings and goings and checked student IDs.

Sears was at the corner of Fordham and Webster. South of Sears there was a Carvel's, and just across from Sears was the North End Liquor Mart. Nearby was a music store where I bought a guitar that I never did learn to play, but it seemed like the thing to do at the time. East of Sears, under the El just south of Fordham Road, there was another bar that attracted Fordham students. It was in a wooden building. Eventually it and an adjacent pet store were closed due to a fire. I happened to walk by one day and saw the corpse of a monkey behind the blackened window; the poor creature was seated with paws covering its head, hiding from a disaster it could not escape.

Going east on Fordham there was a car dealership with plate-glass windows; when we passed by at night, ferocious German shepherds leapt at the windows and made them shake. Past Roosevelt High School was White Castle, a great attraction, especially very late at night. The burgers were inexpensive, and it was tempting to eat too many of them. The shakes were good. For a while they had a very good cheese Danish with grapes in the filling. An interesting combination, but quite tasty.

Halfway through my junior year, I met a young woman at a college dance in the Fordham Rathskeller. She was attending Lehman College and was a friend of someone I had met in a sociology class. We danced and talked and I found out that she came from the old neighborhood: 141st and Willis. Her family had moved to the East Village. We began dating and I began spending a lot of time on the subway. We sometimes met in The Bronx, and often met in Manhattan after work. After taking her home, I faced a long subway ride from 14th Street to Fordham Road. I refined the art of sleeping on the train and waking up at exactly my stop. I only missed once: I woke up but thought I was at 183rd Street. I wasn't. The doors closed. I got off at Kingsbridge, crossed over to the downtown side, and waited for the train to reach Woodlawn and change directions. The conductor probably was not expecting someone to be boarding at two or three in the morning, so the doors opened for just a second. It was the closest to decapitation I ever want to come. But my three years of commuting to Clinton trained me to deal with fast doors and quick-wristed conductors, so I wrestled my way in. I knew to exit quickly when we stopped at Fordham Road.

During my first two years at Fordham, I had completed most of the math, science, theology, philosophy, and history requirements, so as an upperclassman I was able to concentrate on English courses. Since it had become obvious to me that I was never going to learn to play the guitar, I enrolled in a poetry-writing workshop. Creative writing was taught by Marguerite Young, author of *Miss MacIntosh, My Darling,* an epic stream-of-consciousness novel of 1198 pages that took her seventeen years to write. Her comment on the first poem I submitted was effectively brief: "Rubbish." Marguerite was a great presence who told stories of writers and eccentrics. She often wore a paisley coat with a button that alternated between the slogan "All the way with Adlai" and a photograph of the former presidential candidate. Once she had an umbrella strapped around her elbow and did not bother to remove it when she wrote on the board. I took six workshops with her.

It was around this time that The Bronx Council on the Arts opened a storefront on 184th Street, just around the corner from my apartment. They offered a poetry workshop and I joined up. The sessions were facilitated by Ruth Lisa Schechter, a poet who also worked as a poet-therapist. She was kind and nurturing to us novices. Across the street from the BCA was a laundromat. I sometimes helped Mom by taking the wash. One afternoon, while watching the clothes spin around in the dryer, I composed what I thought was my first good poem. It was about my family, and the shoeshine parlor, and The Bronx, subjects I would continue to explore in future years. Unlike Poe Cottage, this literary landmark no longer remains; the laundromat was destroyed by a gas explosion after I moved from New York. For the next two decades, my mother did her laundry the old-fashioned way: with a washboard in the kitchen sink.

At the outset of my senior year, I was planning to apply to graduate school at Fordham. Then one November night we got mugged. Fortunately, we were not hurt, physically. But this was a turning point. I spent the next couple of months applying to out-of-state graduate schools. I told one of my professors, whom I knew fairly well because I had taken several courses with him, what happened and how I was trying to leave New York. He introduced me to another professor who, though he did not know me, discussed the pros and cons of various universities. He recommended Madison as being a nice place to live. The last school I applied to was the University of Wisconsin–Madison. It was the first to respond. I was offered a fellowship, and I accepted.

A few weeks after graduation, my wife and I were married at Saint Jean Baptiste Church. My boss said the mass and performed the ceremony. The next day we flew to Wisconsin. We bought bicycles, which we needed for transportation, as neither of us could drive, and fishing poles. We enjoyed our new life, but with both of our families in New York, we were still tied to the old. We worried about those we left behind.

As the 1970s flowed into the 1980s, life in the city seemed to grow more difficult. The Woodlawn train became known as "The Muggers' Express," and my father started taking the D train home at night. The South Bronx, now an epithet for urban blight, extended up to Fordham Road. Crime surged, and I remember the stories of stores closing early on Halloween to avoid being robbed by people in masks. Drug sales occurred right on the street, in broad daylight, so much so that Mom stopped looking out the window to avoid any repercussions if there happened to be a bust. On one visit home we saw Curtis Sliwa on Fordham Road. He was toting a black plastic garbage bag as he was part of a group attempting to reduce litter in the area. The Guardian Angels, which he founded, patrolled the Woodlawn train, and I know my parents appreciated this effort to protect the public.

As for myself, I avoided subways and took cabs. Many drivers did not want to go to The Bronx. Some refused outright; some gave in after I explained the route and assured them that they could quickly get out of The Bronx and back to Manhattan: make a left at Fordham and zip over to the Deegan or the Harlem River Drive. After we had children, we occasionally used the strategy of putting them in the cab first and negotiating later. This ploy was best executed at LaGuardia Airport, where there was so much traffic that the likelihood of the driver kidnapping the kids and speeding off was greatly diminished. The most enjoyable rides were with older drivers who had once lived in the area. We could talk about the good old days. In one ride down the Grand Concourse, I was shocked to see the boarded-up buildings. Years later I was pleased to see renovation and a new life for these beautiful edifices.

After my father died in the mid-1980s, I hoped to get Mom to move to Wisconsin. But she most certainly did not want to leave The Bronx. How could she leave Alexander's? The store continued to offer bargains. On one visit my wife bought a full-length denim dress for two dollars. Two dollars! You could not beat the price at a thrift store. Mom shopped throughout the year, and at Christmas we received boxes of her trophies: shirts, blouses, kids' clothes, and toys. All carefully and lovingly wrapped.

Mom also did not want to leave her sister, who had finally moved from 138th Street into an apartment on the same floor as Mom, but on the other side of the building, which had two staircases. Another sister moved from 138th Street to Mosholu Parkway, and was not far away from their brother who lived on Bainbridge Avenue. The sisters got together in Mom's living room to knit. They formed their own little garment factory, and we began receiving all manners and sizes of hand-made sweaters. Mom even crocheted outfits for Barbie dolls. She made Cabbage Patch dolls and made so many plastic canvas Christmas ornaments that we did not need anything else but a few lights to decorate our tree. The five-and-tens sold hobby items, and Mom probably got a lot of good bargains as the stores on Fordham Road closed. The livable space in my old bedroom got smaller as Mom's hobby inventory expanded.

Mom had a strong sense of family, and when her brother lost his sight, she often took the bus to Bainbridge Avenue on Saturdays and cleaned his apartment. The years took their toll, and eventually Mom and the sister who lived on Morris Avenue were the last alive of eleven siblings. They spent their days together, had lunch, went shopping, ate an early dinner, and were safely home by nightfall.

I started visiting more frequently, taking my daughter at Christmas and my son at Easter. I tried to avoid summers because of the heat. There was no air conditioning and we did not leave the windows open at night. Though the streets were still crowded with shoppers, the stores on Fordham Road had changed. Alexander's closed, became Caldor's, and Caldor's closed. The five-and-tens were gone. Grant's became Rock Bottom and then became Duane Reade. Modell's took the Woolworth's site. We went there often looking for good deals on Yankees gear. The Dollar Savings Bank was now Emigrant, and the clock no longer worked. Electronic games and Walkmen were popular, so the Wiz was an attraction. Near it was a toy store where my son bought his first skateboard.

One January the East Coast was hit with a major snowstorm. My daughter and I put on our Wisconsin clothes and took a walk. We were in a dollar store on the Concourse when a guy came in and asked the clerk if they sold snow blowers or shovels. At a dollar store? Really? Unlike Madison, which has a fleet of salters, bulldozers, and graders, New York City seemed to deal with the snow by attaching plows to sanitation trucks. So until most of the snow was removed, the garbage continued to pile up on Morris Avenue. Finally, at nine o'clock on a Saturday night, I heard a familiar drone and looked out the window to see the garbage being collected.

I have learned, through experience, that digging out a car that has been plowed in is not fun. So I watched with great interest as a man extricated his car from a snowed-in parking spot. I did not see him use a shovel. He continually burned rubber until the car slid out without hitting the cars parked in front and behind his. He was either extremely talented or extremely lucky. When I called the airline to ask if our return flight had been delayed, the woman sheepishly told me that it had been cancelled. She was surprised at my joy. I told her that I did not mind being stuck at Mom's house, but I did not want to be stuck at LaGuardia. It was probably the only happy phone call she got that day.

When we did fly back, our flight left on schedule. But we spent two and a half hours on the tarmac in Detroit; they did not have a terminal available. We had to remain in our seats, because the plane might move at any time. Which it did not. It was maddening. After that, I avoided Detroit by taking Midwest Airlines. If I got stuck I would either be in Milwaukee, where I could take a bus home, or in LaGuardia, where I could take a cab to Mom's. Midwest had comfortable seats, decent meals, and they gave you a cookie.

I never really enjoyed travelling and sometimes pretended that the plane was just a subway car. I was just starting to get more comfortable when 9/11 happened and air travel took on a new dimension. On one return trip, in the spring of 2002, my son and I were sitting in the passenger area waiting for our flight. There was an armed National Guardsman on our side of the security checkpoint. He left briefly to get a cup of coffee. On his return, coffee in hand, the woman at the checkpoint asked to see his ID. A woman in a blue blazer asking a guy in camo with an automatic weapon strapped to his shoulder for his ID. That's chutzpah!

On the morning of 9/11, I was talking on the phone with Mom. She told me a plane had struck the World Trade Center. She did not seem too concerned. She probably assumed it was a small plane, and she remembered the B-25 crashing into the Empire State Building in 1945. As I drove off to teach my morning classes, I listened to the car radio and learned what had happened. There were televisions in our classrooms, and we saw the towers collapse. During my free period I called my mother-in-law who lived on 12th Street. She could smell the smoke, but was okay. The following spring my son and I visited Ground Zero. We will never feel what those living in New York City felt when this happened, but we will never forget what we saw.

A few months later, just after the school semester ended, I received a call from Mom's doctor. Mom had some health problems and would be in the hospital for a short time. I flew out the next day. Alone. Afraid. This was a different visit. My aunt no longer lived in the building; she was in a nursing home. When I got to the apartment, there was no Mom looking out the window waiting for the cab to pull up. No Mom to unlock the door and greet me. No Mom to ask what I wanted for dinner.

Mom was in Beth Israel North. She had a room overlooking Gracie Mansion. There was a wonderful view of the Hell Gate, Mill Rock, and Wards Island. These were all places that fascinated me as a child, and I spent much time gazing out the window. It was a peaceful diversion from the numbing stress of sitting in a hospital room worrying about Mom's health. People were fishing from a boat off Wards Island; what could they be tying to catch? Was the East River coming back to life?

The short hospital stay lasted over a week. I lived on a diet of canned tuna and canned beans, supplemented by sandwiches from the deli near the hospital. My Boy Scout training had taught me to "be prepared," and over the years I had stashed extra clothes, extra underwear, and other essentials in my old bedroom. The other essentials consisted of a carton of cigarettes and a couple of small bottles of brandy, both of which disappeared rather quickly. The cigarettes were fairly replaceable, although if bought at the wrong store they were not always fresh. The brandy, however, was different. This was not just any brandy; it was Korbel. Wisconsin may be famous for its beer, but it is also the greatest consumer of Korbel brandy. And there I was: a Badger in The Bronx and running out of brandy.

So on one of my hospital visits, I took a cigarette break and sought out liquor stores. There were plenty, and cognac and all sorts of exotic refreshments were available. But no Korbies. I walked on, and eventually found a store that carried it. I purchased two bottles. Of course, I still had to go back and finish my visit with Mom. There was a security guard at the front desk, and I did not think he would take too kindly to my carrying liquor into a hospital. I was wearing a Levi's denim jacket, and found that each inside pocket was large enough to hold a liter bottle. I kept my arms at my sides to make the bulge less visible as I walked past the guard. On the cab ride home, I cradled the bottles and hoped we would not hit too many bumps on the Deegan.

It was a relief to get Mom home. She required a lot of care: changing bandages, weekly injections, and doctors' appointments. My initial plan was to clean the apartment and to make it easier for her to take care of. It was overrun with roaches. It was not her fault. She kept it as clean as she could. I talked to the neighbors; it seemed that everybody's apartments were overrun. I washed the dishes after we ate, and again before we used them. One of her medical appointments was at a luxury building on 72nd Street where an exterminator was attempting to eliminate "water bugs" (two-inch long American cockroaches). At least we did not have "water bugs."

I thought if I caulked the spaces around the toilet and gas meter, I could reduce the bug problem. So one evening, I headed down to Sears, the only hardware merchant I could think of. I bought a couple of tubes of caulk, and when I exited, I looked across Webster Avenue. There it was. The Pennywhistle and Pick and Shovel were gone. The Third Avenue El was no more. But after twenty-eight years the liquor store had endured. How could I resist. I opened the door and looked around. There it was, in the middle of the store: a pyramid of Korbel proudly displayed! I came, I saw, I purchased. For the next month, every Friday night I made my pilgrimage.

Mom would eventually need dialysis, and her eyesight was failing. My cousin had been taking her to her doctor appointments, and a friend had been taking her grocery shopping, but her needs were growing greater, and I could not take care of her long-distance. I began a campaign to get her to move in with us. She finally agreed. Instead of repairing the apartment, I began disassembling it. I took care of her and sorted stuff with her during the day, but could not pack boxes until ten or eleven at night when she went to bed. The place was stifling hot, and only after a few nightcaps could I get to sleep at two or three in the morning.

Most of the moving companies I called would not help us. They dealt only with main routes to Chicago or Miami. I finally found a company in Queens that was willing to store the stuff for a month then put it in a semi headed for Minneapolis. I packed box after box until there was just a narrow path through the living room. The movers came and took over two hundred items. There was still plenty more stuff, and I sent as much as I could by UPS or US Mail. I had no choice but to leave the rest.

I did not know when I would be done packing, so I waited until the last possible minute to call for a plane ticket. My goal was to be back in Madison for my son's birthday. I called the airline late on a Friday night and purchased two one-way tickets to Madison for Sunday. Mom and I had breakfast that Sunday morning, then we finished packing. Two suitcases of clothes. Two duffel bags of valuables, as well as last minute items like the coffee pot and cups. I tied twenty or so knots on the duffel bags. Any potential thief could quickly open a suitcase lock, but would he or she have the time to untie all those knots?

I called for a cab early, and hoped that we could make our exit from The Bronx by way of the Concourse and across 138th Street. The driver did not want to do this, and I did not have the energy to debate him, so we did the Deegan and Triborough route to LaGuardia. We arrived quite early. This turned out to be good. There was a star on each of our tickets: we had been selected to be thoroughly searched.

The lady was nice to Mom as she carefully wanded the metal clasps of her undergarment. I was wanded, then taken to a special room. I stood in the center of it and our two suitcases and two duffel bags were set upon four tables, one on each side of the room. All of the knots were untied. Everything was unpacked. The two ladies giggled when the coffee pot came rolling out. At another table, my suitcase lay, still unopened. The man called to me in a shrill voice.

I am pretty good at understanding dialect, but I had no idea what he was saying, so of course he said it louder and angrier. Finally, it became clear that he wanted me to unlock the suitcase. It was not locked, so I went over and simply snapped the button open. The ladies laughed. The man did not share their humor.

After we landed in Milwaukee, I thought I would save some time, so I went to security and told them that we were the lucky people who get to be searched. But they had no interest in searching us. An hour later we landed in Madison, and I was reunited with my wife and children. The kids were delighted that their Grandma was moving in.

Mom lived with us for eleven years, and spent nine years going to dialysis three times a week. Watching her accept the long needles being inserted into her forearm made me admire her courage. Mom's commitment to her family continued over the years, and she spent many hours on the phone talking to her friends and to her nieces. She had a schedule of who to call, at what time, on what day. The phone bill logged three-to-four thousand minutes a month. We had unlimited long distance so that was fine with us. She loved talking about the good old days and keeping up with the latest goings-on.

After Mom died, we had a service in Madison, then returned to New York. We stayed at a hotel on the Upper East Side. I knew the area, so it was like a second home. We visited St. Jean's almost everyday for daily mass. The new Monsignor remembered my former boss. I even got to talk to one of the ladies who used to work in the office with me. These were comforting connections in a stressful time. We had a service for the family at Sisto Funeral Home on East Tremont. Sisto had buried my grandparents, my father, and several other relatives. They were very helpful to Mom when Dad died, and, twenty-five years later, they were once again very helpful as my wife and I completed the arrangements for Mom's burial.

The family came, from The Bronx, from upstate New York, Rhode Island, and Florida. I was touched by their loyalty to my mother. Mom is buried next to Dad in Saint Raymond's Cemetery. The old section. Not far from her sister. Not far from her parents, brother, and nephews.

We had a few extra days in the city. We went to the East Village and Brooklyn to see my wife's family, and we got to do a bit of sightseeing. When I took the kids to New York, I never managed to get to the Metropolitan Museum of Art until two or three o'clock, which did not give us much time to see everything. On one trip I rushed my daughter through room after room of the Picasso exhibit. This time, my wife and I spent most of the day there. We also went to the Whitney, which I had often visited because it was so close to where I worked. And we went to the Museum of Modern Art where we spent much time gazing at Van Gogh's *Starry Night*. We walked around the Upper East Side and ate at the Second Avenue Deli, which was now at the corner of 75th Street and First Avenue. My brother-in-law walked us around the East Village to show us how it had gentrified. He showed us the site of the original Second Avenue Deli, which had the names of Jewish movie stars inscribed in the sidewalk.

There was one attraction I wanted to visit before our return to Madison. There was a Wisconsin bar on Third Avenue. According to local gossip, the bar once got in trouble for selling Spotted Cow beer. Spotted Cow is made in New Glarus, Wisconsin, and why the brewery does not want its products sold out-of-state, I do not know. But I have hosted visitors who would buy a case before returning to the Twin Cities. I wanted to visit this bar and enjoy a brandy. The establishment had a familiar "Motion W" flag and a Yankees flag. It seemed to be the place to go to watch a Badger football game or a Yankees game. The waitress, who was from Texas, was most pleasant. They did have brandy, but they did not have Korbel. I ordered, and thoroughly enjoyed, a club soda. We went back to the hotel and I had a nightcap. I had come prepared. It was Korbel.

At the end of the week, we returned to Madison; we were both relieved that we had fulfilled Mom's final wish to be buried beside her husband.

I am grateful that she was able to be with us for so many years. The house is so quiet without her.

Publications by W. R. Rodriguez

Books in Print

from the banks of brook avenue. Zeugpress, 2016.
the shoe shine parlor poems et al: second edition. Zeugpress, 2016.
concrete pastures of the beautiful bronx. Zeugpress, 2008.
the shoe shine parlor poems et al. Ghost Pony Press, 1984.

E-publications: Zeugpress/Smashwords Editions

the bronx trilogy. 2017.
from the banks of brook avenue: annotated edition. 2017.
The Bronx: Three Memoirs. 2016.
the shoe shine parlor poems et al: second edition. 2016.
from the banks of brook avenue. 2015.
concrete pastures of the beautiful bronx. 2014.
The Shoe Shine Parlor Poems et al: A Teacher's Guide. 2014.
the shoe shine parlor poems et al (first edition). 2014.

E-publications are available at:

www.smashwords.com/profile/view/wrrodriguez

For more information, or to listen to recordings of the author reading his poetry, visit his web site at:

http://www.wrrodriguez.com

www.ingramcontent.com/pod-product-compliance
Lightning Source LLC
Chambersburg PA
CBHW070942160426
43193CB00011B/1777